The

Staffordshire Bull Terrier

OTHER TITLES

STAFFORDSHIRE BULL TERRIER Jack Barnard 978-1-85736- 350-0
First President of Club. Traces the early development. A Classic Reprint

STAFFORDSHIRE BULL TERRIER   H N Beilby 978-1-85736-083-7
A scientific approach to the Standard and different lines. Probably the leading title on the development and understanding of the breed. A Classic Reprint

STAFFORDSHIRE BULL TERRIER Joseph Dunn   978-1-85736-355-5
Joe Dunn, as he was known, was the pioneer responsible for getting recognition of the breed by the Kennel Club. A Classic Reprint

STAFFORDSHIRE BULL TERRIERS MajoCount V C Hollender
978-1-85736-123-0   History and a collection of chapters by the leading pioneers such as Jack Barnard, John F Gordon, Joe Mallen, W A Boylan and A W A Cairns. A Classic Reprint

STAFFORDSHIRE BULL TERRIERS –In History & Sport
              Mike Homan 978-1-85259-078-5
Traces the history from early times and covers the present day dog.

STAFFORDSHIRE BULL TERRIERS – Irish and English Shaun Barker
           978-1-85736-242-8 (cased) & 243-5 (Limp)
A new critical study of the English Staffordshire and comparing it with the Irish which is more like the older type of the breed.

THE AMERICAN PIT BULL TERRIER & HIS MASTER   L B HANNA
1SBN 978- 1-85736-462-0   A Classic Reprint

THE BULLDOG –A Monograph Edgar Farman 978-1-85736-260-2
A massive history of the development of the bulldog from early times, covering the old time bulldog and its emergence as a show dog.   ?

THE BULL DOG   Robert Fulton   978-1-85736-568-9
A new edition of a very rare book. The author is famous for his massive book on pigeons, but he was also an expert on Bulldogs

THE ENGLISH BULLDOG A History Joseph Batty 978-1-85736-567-2
An analysis of the known history of the English Bulldog from early times, including possible links with the Mastiff and other breeds. The origins of the Bulldog and the old, now illegal sports associated with the breed. Evolution from the fearless warrior to the show dog of today. Has the developme

BULLDOG BREEDING FOR BEGINNERS Vicky Collins-Nattrass
978-1-85736-574-0
A guide for all who wish to consider breeding bulldogs. It is quite comprehensive and covers likely problems.

BULL TERRIERS & HOW TO BREED THEM   (A Classic Reprint)
Richard H Glyn ISBN 978-1-85736-407-4
 Early history of blood sports, development of bull terriers in a backround of violence against animals. Selection and breeding. Old dog champions.

The

Staffordshire

Bull Terrier

Jack Barnard

First President: Staffordshire Bull Terrier Club

Beech Publishing House

7 Station Yard
Elsted Marsh
Midhurst
West Sussex GU29 0JT

ISBN 978-1-85736-350-0

A Classic Reprint
1990, 1997, 2007

British Library Cataloguing-in-Publication Data
A catalogue record for this book is available
from the British Library.

Beech Publishing House
Station Yard
Elsted Marsh
Midhurst
West Sussex GU29 OJT

FOREWORD

The Staffordshire Bull Terrier has not been written in competition with the numerous books on dogs.

It is intended as a concise and complete guide for expert and novice alike, introducing to all, the merit of the "King of the Canine World"., as such it is complete.

Each page is a mine of information and has been written with great thought by one who was cradled in the complex task of breeding, and fixing type so that the gamest of terriers could be recognized at a glance.

The author, in unwasted words has collected facts, principal facts, practical facts, and facts from long personal experience.

In addition no source of authentic information has been missed, and the results of the search is presented in a handy form for the self instruction of the reader.

ALFRED JONES ARPS
Hon. Sec. Potteries Bull Breeds Society, etc.

PUBLISHER'S FOREWORD

Although the text has been typeset to improve quality some of the original illustrations are still of poor quality and for this we apologize.

Jack Barnard

The Staffordshire Bull Terrier Club's First President

Breeder, Exhibitor, Exporter
& Specialist Judge
& All-Rounder all Breeds

THE STAFFORDSHIRE BULL TERRIER

IT is an acknowledged fact that of all animals the Dog holds the premier position as man's most faithful companion and servant. Indeed, as a servant the usefulness of dogs tends to increase. By careful breeding man has succeeded in developing a wide variety of types, and there are now dogs specially suited to supply man's individual requirements in a hundred different ways.

There are dogs peculiarly bred to be pets. There are also dogs bred with infinite care to be an invaluable ally of man when game hunting and shooting. There is the sheep dog, without those services the difficult task of sheep farming in mountainous areas would be impossible. There are dogs that will guard man's possessions in face of every opposition. Indeed, in whatever sphere man's activities may be engaged - sport, pleasure, war, industry, commerce, or ordinary domestic life the dog always has and always will find a sure and certain place.

While acknowledging all the natural qualities possessed by the dog, it has to be admitted that much of his present intellect and many of his moral characteristics have been carefully fostered by man. By means of constant companionship, patient training, and scientific breeding, dogs have been produced that are as mentally alert as they are physically perfect. The general public are indebted to we breeders, who are continually striving to improve the qualities of man's most faithful friend and servant, which sometimes is a most difficult problem. In the British Isles, in particular, the work of breeders has been carried out with unfailing enthusiasm and devotion. Many difficulties and problems have had to be overcome, but thanks to unremitting labour and constant study, British dog breeding has reached a very high standard of efficiency. Therefore dog lovers who desire to own a dog that will prove a true, staunch companion and faithful servant will be well advised to purchase a true British product, the Staffordshire Bull Terrier. They will also be well advised to place their requirements in the hands of a reputable breeder. By so doing, they will be showing their appreciation of the work of those responsible for maintaining and improving the high qualities of our most noble breed. We ourselves have always aimed at breeding and trying to produce the very best, to give the public full satisfaction and quality to the last degree.

My idea of compiling this booklet is to try and enlighten and advise the novice, and to give those advice who do not know a true and full description of the Stafford. Although in the eyes of a large majority of the general public, the Staffordshire Bull Terrier is a new breed, yet it may be classed as a very old one.

Two very well-known gentlemen have been very kind to me in allowing me the use of the three blocks in my booklet, "Bull Baiting," "Bear Baiting," and "Dog Fighting" : J. Wentworth Day, Esq. Editor of *The Illustrated Sporting and Dramatic News,* and Walter T. Spencer, Esq., the well-known print dealer, bookseller, and collector of old sporting pictures, of New Oxford Street, London, and I take this opportunity of thanking both for allowing me to enlighten the public with these pictures of some of the old-time so-called sports, and to every lady or gentleman interested in old-time sports. They should not miss the opportunity of reading "A Falcon on St. Paul's," a fascinating record of London's sporting and natural history, by J. Wentworth Day, Esq., price 10/6.

The standard of the Staffordshire Bull Terrier Club was taken from this dog, and the remarks reprinted from *Our Dogs,* 26th April, 1935 issue, are :-"After visiting several kennels of very old breeders of Staffordshire Bull Terriers, I have compiled a standard of points which, in their opinion and mine, is very typical of the breed. The photograph of a brindle and white dog illustrated in this column will give readers some idea of a real Staffordshire.

"This dog is 21/2 years old, stands 171/2 inches at shoulders; circumference of skull, 17 inches; neck 151/2; chest, 261/2 inches; length of back, 16 inches; tail 9 inches; weight, 33 lbs, in hard condition. His breeding can be traced back over 30 years by its present owner - J. DUNN.

2

"JIM THE DANDY"

One of the most typical dogs of the fancy,

owned by Barnard Bros.

The Type and Standard was taken from this Dog and accepted

by the Staffordshire Bull Terrier Club at its formation in 1935.

No breed of dog is at present making such a typical advance in public favour as the modern and improved Staffordshire Bull Terrier, and its well deserved popularity seems far more likely to be permanent than that of other breeds which have in turn been taken up, only to be dismissed by their owners when their lack of intelligence, cowardice, or general inutility has proved them to be unworthy of the patronage bestowed upon them.

This dog, in its turn, was brought into existence by crossing the Bull Dog and the Terrier, and was produced in the first instance by the supporters and lovers of dog fighting, who wished to obtain a longer and more punishing head than the Bull Dog. This cross in the first instance produced a sullen-looking, thick-skulled dog, showing slight indications of symmetry in its composition, but still an ideal specimen of dog for the purpose for which he was called into existence.

One of the earliest records of Bull Terriers to be found is Blaine's *Rural Sport*, in which allusion is made to the breed in the following words - "A large breed of English terriers has of late sprung up. These by being crossed with the bull dog have gained undaunted courage in attacking the higher order of vermin, as the badger etc."

In the *Naturalist's Library*, too, by Sir William Jardine, published 1843, it is thus alluded to - "In England the cross of terriers is perceptible in sheep and cattle dogs, but most of all in the breed called bull terriers, because it is formed of these two varieties, and constitutes the most determined and savage race known".

The size of the Stafford is given in a later page, and thus admirers of the breed have the opportunity of selecting a dog whose size is adapted for the work or kennel accommodation at hand.

Though his extreme courage and intelligence render this breed of dog eminently qualified for an indoor dog, few varieties require more genuine hard work and outdoor exercise to get them into show condition, as the muscles which should be so plainly visible on the fore and hind quarters of a dog in perfect condition become relaxed and flabby if his proper amount of exercise is curtailed.

4

To those who reside in towns, or have not the proper time to give to exercising, might I suggest that by chasing a ball for two hours a day, morning and night, in the garden or any spare land that may be at hand, or if possible, to hang a piece of cat skin on a wall or at the end of a stick, and keeping it out of the dog's reach, they will create exercise that the dog would never get, in trying to obtain possession of the treasure by jumping up at it. These methods of exercising a dog in a small space may, perhaps, be novel to readers who are well situated for space.

A very silly prejudice exists against the Stafford, on account of his alleged ferocity of temper and irresistible inclination to fight all other dogs that he comes in contact with. Thus, many would-be-supporters of this noble breed have held aloof from it in consequence of the reports heard. There may be a slight foundation for the detractions, I cannot deny, applying to the minority, which can apply to any breed, but after a considerable experience of these dogs I unhesitatingly affirm that the prejudice against his temper is grossly exaggerated, unless purposely bred for the specific reason of fighting and killing, which years ago was a common sport in England. No breed of dog, if properly brought up and kindly treated, is more susceptible to affection towards his master, and docility and intelligence are properties which are highly developed in a Stafford. Naturally, a dog which may be said to be a born gladiator possesses a greater amount of courage and tenacity in his attack than animals of a gentler temperament.

As a gentleman's companion, in town or country, the Stafford is unapproached. He is a handsome fellow to look at if kept in proper condition, affectionate, and a true staunch pal. It is, however, for his indomitable courage that the Stafford is so highly prized by many, for, though usually mute like the bull dog, his system of attack is different from the latter. Instead of hanging on to his antagonist, he will tear him to pieces, and his pluck is so great that he is able to endure an enormous amount of punishment, whilst in his turn he is managing his foe with his powerful jaws.

That the Staffordshire Bull Terrier is a dog of very long standing is proved by the facts of records and very old prints which established his existence in the eighteenth century.

For a period of well over a hundred years this breed of dog has been associated with many of the barbarous sports indulged in by our forefathers. Bull rings and bull stakes may today be seen in Birmingham and their neighbouring Black Country, which bear evidence to the existence of these amusements in the district in the past.

Bull baiting, bear baiting, dog fighting, and other blood sports all fell to his lot, with the result that between 1850 and 1870, when dog breeding began to assume serious proportions, our breed was regarded as disreputable and did not receive encouragement. Chiefly miners and ironworkers in Staffordshire and other localities preserved the breed, together with the qualities of gameness and intelligence which the breed is justified in receiving.

To a large extent the Stafford has always been a constant pal to the working man, especially in the Black Country. Undoubtedly a born fighter, he is in ordinary life a docile and intelligent companion. The intelligence of the adult Stafford is high, but I may say it takes some eighteen to twenty-four months before he reaches full maturity. Up to twelve months or so he is not so intelligent, but later his mental development is very rapid.

A meeting was called on 25th May, 1935, which was held at the Cross Guns Hotel, Cradley Heath, South Staffs., with the specific purpose of forming a club. Some forty to fifty gentlemen breeders and owners attended, amongst them being Mr. Alf. Garrett, whose family has bred Staffordshires for over eighty years. It was decided to call the club "The Original Staffordshire Bull Terrier Club," but this was not accepted by Kennel Club, the title chosen being "The Staffordshire Bull Terrier Club." Might I mention that I had the honour of being elected the Club's first President. The Committee is composed of eight well-known local gentlemen who have been breeding Staffordshires for twenty to fifty years.

It was decided to fix the annual member's subscription at 5/- per member, and joint partners 7/6. Several dogs of good type were on view here for the purpose of giving everyone some idea of the type that is wanted, the type and standard laid down by the Club being accepted by Kennel Club.

6

GREAT HERTFORDSHIRE OPEN SHOW AT HATFIELD, JUNE 20th, 1935.

Mr. S. Crabtree (third from right) judging Staffordshire Bull Terriers.
This was the first time they had been classified since their recognition by the Kennel Club.
Photo : J. H. Moore, N.10.

The standard laid down by the Staffordshire Bull Terrier Club is as follows:-

The Staffordshire Bull Terrier is a smooth-coated dog, standing between 15 and 18 inches at the shoulder. He should give the impression of great strength for his size and, although muscular, should possess two necessary qualifications which have a very important bearing on this breed of dog, especially if out for sport, and these are activity and agility.

The head should be short, deep through, broad skull and very pronounced cheek muscles, distinct stop, short foreface with a level mouth. Ears : Rose, Half-rose and prick. These three to be preferred; full drop to be penalised. Years ago it was common custom to crop the ears of this breed, but owing to the laws of this country this practice was abolished. Eye to be dark. Body : Short back, deep brisket, light in loins with forelegs set rather wide apart to permit of chest development. The front legs should be straight, feet well padded to turn out a little and showing no weakness at pasterns. Hind legs : Hindquarters well muscled, let down at hocks like a terrier. Coat : Short, smooth and close to skin. Tail : The tail should be of medium length, tapering to a point and carried rather low. It should not curl much, and may be compared to an old-fashioned pump handle.

The weight of a dog should be from 28 to 38 lbs., and the weight of a bitch 24 - 34 lbs. Colour may be any shade of Brindle consisting of Black, White, Fawn or Red, or any of these colours, with White, Black-and-Tan, and Liver not to be encouraged.

The faults to be penalised are :- Dudley nose; light or pink eyes; tail too long or badly curled; undershot and overshot mouths.

As stated, the size of the Stafford is moderate, but he is large enough to be an excellent guard for either the house or property, for the motorist an unapproachable parking attendant, and when full and properly trained will await his master's return for hours, quietly and silently guarding the car from all comers.

Now the size and standard have been given, allow me to give a little advice to intending breeders as to the value of kindness towards their stock. Do not be frightened of the dogs, don't knock them about or ill-use them, and no breed of dog will treat his master with greater respect than will the game, handsome, intelligent and loveable Staffordshire Bull Terrier.

8

ARTICLES OF AGREEMENT
USED IN THE DAYS OF DOG FIGHTING

Articles of Agreement made on the ....
day of .... 18 ....
.... agrees
to fight his ....dog ....pound
weight against .... dog
....,..... pounds
weight, for £ ....aside at ....
on the ....day of ....18.
The dogs to be weighed at ....o'clock in
the .... and fight between ....
o'clock in the ....

The deposits to be made as is hereinafter mentioned; to be delivered to
....
(who is to be the final Stakeholder), namely, the first deposit of £...................
aside at the making of the match; the Second Deposit of £................. aside, on
the .... of ....at the house of
....; Third Deposit of
£.........................on the ....
of ....at the house of ....;
Fourth Deposit of £ ....on the ....
of ....at the house of ....
....and the Fifth Deposit of £ ....
on the .... of ....at
the house of ....;
which is the last.

RULES

1st - To be a fair fight   yards from the scratch.

2nd - Both dogs to be tasted before and after fighting   if required.

3rd - Both dogs to be shewn fair to the scratch, and washed at their own corners.

4th - Both seconds to deliver the Dogs fair from the corner, and not leave until the Dogs commence fighting.

5th - A Referee to be chosen in the pit; one minute time to be allowed between every fair go away; fifty seconds allowed for sponging; and at the expiration of that time the time-keeper shall call make ready, and as soon as the minute is expired the Dogs to be delivered, and the Dog refusing or stopping on the way to be the Loser.

6th - Should either second pick up his dog in a mistake, he shall put it down immediately, by order of the Referee, or the money to be forfeited.

9

7th - Should anything pernicious be found on either Dog, before or after fighting in the pit, the backers of the Dog so found to forfeit, and the person holding the battle money to give it up immediately, when called upon to do so.

8th - Referee to be chosen in the pit before fighting, whose decision in all cases shall be final.

9th - Either dog exceeding the stipulated weight, on the day of weighing, to forfeit the money deposited.

10th - In any case of a Dog being declared dead by the Referee, the living dog shall remain at him for ten minutes when he shall be taken to his corner if it be his turn to scratch or if it be the dead Dogs turn the Fight shall be at an end by order of the Referee.

11th - In any case of Police interference the Referee to name the next place and time of fighting, on the same day if possible and day by day until it be decided, but if no Referee be chosen, the Stake holder to name the next place and time; but if a Referee has been chosen and then refuses to name the next place and time of fighting, or goes away after being disturbed, then the power of choosing the next time and place be left with the Stakeholder and a fresh Referee to be chosen in the pit, and the power of the former one to be entirely gone.

12th - In case of Police interference and the dogs have commenced fighting they will not be required to weigh any more; but if they have not commenced fighting they will have to weigh day by day at ___ lbs. until decided at the time and place named by the Referee, or if he refuses or goes away then the Stakeholder has to name the time and place.

13th - The seconder of either Dog is upon no consideration to call his adversary's Dog by name while in the pit, nor use anything whatever in his hands with which to call of his Dog.

14th - To toss up the night before fighting for the place of fighting, between the hours of ___ and ___ o'clock at the house where the last deposit is made.

15th - The above stakes are not to be given up until fairly won or lost by a fight, unless either party break the above agreement.

16th - All deposits to be made between the hours of and ___ o'clock at night.

17th - Either party not following up or breaking the above agreement to forfeit the money down.

....

....

....

....

Witnesses .... Signed ....

....

10

"THE WESTMINSTER DOG PIT." From a scarce colour drawing, "Designed by an amateur." By courtesy of Mr. W. T. Spencer. Also by courtesy of J. Wentworth Day, Esq., author of "A Falcon on St. Paul's" (Hutchinson, price 10/6).

INTERESTING EVENTS OF BYGONE DAYS.
BULL BAITING AT ROWLEY REGIS.

The note on Bull Baiting at Hales Owen (No. 2037) has caused much talk. Men much older than myself say it was all true, and much worse than has been described. They tell me they have stood among the crowd and seen not only the dog hoisted up high in the air, but that often, when the bull had the first chance, he would meet the dog and put his foot on him and kill him on the spot. And if a man owned a dog which would not face the bull, he would kick him most shamefully and send him off yoicking. A few young people are rather incredulous about it, and for their information I would like to give a few facts from others older. I am informed on good authority that bull baiting prevailed very extensively in the parish of Rowley Regis. Old people declare it true that on one occasion, the Rev. George Sarrs, who was curate for the parish for 40 years, once went into the crowd at the baiting to do his best to put a stop to the baiting, and one of the leaders struck him on the face, knocking out some of his teeth. He entered the ministry in 1800, and in his memoirs he says, "The horrid practice of bull baiting here prevailed with all its revolting aggravations, and to their shame be it recorded, received countenance and support from many who considered themselves far from the vulgar rabble." Cock fighting, bear baiting, and every other species of wickedness formed the popular amusements of the day.

HALES OWEN.

JAMES ADAMS

(Reprinted from the "Birmingham Post",
December 1886, and February 1887).

(2037) BULL BAITING AT HALES OWEN

As an interested reader of this column, by your permission I will add a note on the old and barbarous custom of bull baiting, which I witnessed in my youth. I am 56 years old, and can well remember, opposite my home, a bull being baited year after year. I was only a little village called Gorsty Hill, near Hales Owen. My home stood high on a bank, so that I could see over the heads of the crowds, with their dogs barking and struggling to fight the bull. I could see the bull in the centre of the mob. Sometimes the bull would throw the dog up in the air like a child would throw a ball. The dog would whirl round and round and fall heavily on the ground, or among the people. At other times the dog would pin the bull by the nose or between the hind legs, causing the bull to roar and rave about in great agony. It was frightful for us young people to hear

"BULL BROKE LOOSE." An unexpected incident in a Bull Bait at Barnett Fair.
By courtesy of Mr. W. T. Spencer. Also by courtesy of J. Wentworth Day, Esq.,
author of "A Falcon on St. Paul's" Hutchinson, price 10/6).

and see. Both bull and dogs must have suffered greatly, and the people called it sport or fun.

Let the reader judge for himself. The man in charge of the bull would get help of several of the strongest men as he led the bull into the ring. In spite of all the strength of the men at one end of the chain, the bull would run them about the field. After he had been baited for a time or two, causing such an uproar in all directions, the people scattered hither and thither. I thought these were awful days, the bull roaring, the men swearing, the dogs barking, the children shouting, and the women squealing. After the bull was taken in the mob would push to the other end of the village, where another was brought out for the same purpose, and when that one was taken in the crowd would push back to the other bull- ring, when the former would again be brought out and baited again. The mob would push back all together, as if mad, or move like wild savages, vicious for their prey.

The whole day was spent in this way, and at other games not much better, in running up and down the village in crowds to see the barbarous and shocking sight. The blood would be dropping from the nose and other parts of the bull, and dogs carried in the arms of their owners, with scars of blood and wounds caused by the horns of the bull, or by falling to the ground after being thrown into the air. I have been told that every dog, before he could be permitted to have his bite at the bull, must first be paid for, but I have never been told how much the owner had to pay for his chance, but perhaps some reader may tell.

HALES OWEN.   JAMES OWEN
(Reprinted from the "Birmingham Post",
December 1886, and February 1887,)

I have been informed by an old friend of mine, now eighty years of age, that one of the methods of getting Stafford fighting fit was to obtain a mongrel dog of the terrier type and tie him up short on the far side of a really big fire and allow the fire to become very hot. Tie the Stafford up at the other end with a long elastic rope, just short enough to allow him to slash the other. Leave for about ten minutes and work this up to twenty minutes at the end of the twelfth day, and always allow your dog to kill the mongrel each day. After ten to twelve days of such training, the dog is

14

"BEAR BAITING."

By courtesy of Mr. W. T. Spencer. Also by courtesy of J. Wentworth Day, Esq., author of "A Falcon on St. Paul's" (Hutchinson, price 10 6).

From the painting by Henry Alken.

supposed to be at his best, and during this period he is kept in a pitch dark room and fed on raw meat and blood. They can then be brought out and are ready for the dog pit, and would, I believe, if need be, face a tiger. However, this crude method of dog fighting is outside the British law today, and good riddance.

Dog fighting was more or less a very common sport years ago, and it was no uncommon thing even in the heart of London, just prior to the war, for the old rat and dog pits to be found, and also cock fighting, where these so-called sports took place nightly. And men from all over England would bring their Staffordshire Bulls and rat killers to prove their worth. Dog fighting to a real, true dog lover, would, I should imagine, prove a very sickening affair, especially to see them matched and fight to the death for a few paltry pounds.

Rat killing being a totally different matter, I feel confident every reader of my booklet will agree when I say I have no sympathy for this creature, and anyone who understands his infinite capacity for cruelty, damage, disease, and destruction cannot have the least compunction or feeling where the rat is concerned. I think it ranks amongst the foremost animals as being the most cold-blooded, ferocious, destructive, and disease-carrying animal in the British Isles. Yet to give it credit, it is a born fighter, and I think to watch good dogs kill these vermin is real true sport, it being one of the neatest, slickest things imaginable, the real Stafford being a master of his job.

To see a sackful of rats turned out in a pit and see the leaping, running, squealing mass set upon by the dog is a pleasure, to watch him snapping, shaking, tossing in an unbelievable sequence of speed and movement - one snap, a bite and toss; and its all over. A good dog ought to kill his fifteen rats a minute and, of course, not go to sleep over it.

Dog fighting, the most degrading, brutal and inexcusable sport imaginable, I believe still exists today in some parts of Staffordshire, the mining districts on the Welsh borders, and in one or two instances on the Home Counties. Although this may be carried on to a small extreme, it is a fast-dying so-called sport.

16

REARING, FEEDING AND TRAINING THE PUPPY.

To commence rearing a puppy after weaning is not a difficult task, especially the Staffordshire Bull Terrier. The usual age for them to be sold at varies from six to eight weeks old, this being a nice age, as the small stomachs by this time have become accustomed to digesting foods other than that provided by the dams. Up to three months old I advise about four meals a day, only very small portions being given at a time, and whatever is left, if any, from each meal, never allow it to remain in the kennel or house where the dog is kept, but remove it immediately.

For the morning and evening meal oatmeal gruel or porridge is good. The midday mean consisting of raw minced meat mixed with bread or biscuits, the other meal may consist of a few biscuits. Always allow your puppy to have a large clean uncooked bone; this will help to condition the teeth; and always allow a good supply of clean drinking water, this being an asset to any dog.

If the puppy at eight weeks old has not been successfully wormed, it is advisable to do so without delay, and it should not be left longer than twelve weeks; and the dose should be repeated at four months. It is useless to worm a puppy on a full stomach or to feed after. Always allow at least two hours before feeding, and then give a nice warm soft feed.

Always see that your dogs are housed in nice clean airy kennels. Always allow a nice current of air to run through the kennels, but not to be draughty. Also, always avoid damp, as no dog will thrive in this. Always see that a nice clean straw bed is kept, and the other part of the kennel floor scattered with sawdust; this being cleaned out at least once a day.

PREPARATION FOR SHOW

There are more ways of showing a dog to his best advantage than merely leading him into the ring. The dog should be taught to stand, not in a listless manner, but on the qui vive and showing himself to full advantage. To obtain this result a small piece of boiled or roasted liver is an incentive, as dogs love this.

He should also be taught to walk, trot and gallop on the lead. This should be practised before going into the ring; otherwise, don't expect your dog to shine. I have known scores of dogs to be put down through bad ring manners. No dog shown out of condition has a chance against one properly put down. This remains with the owner to see to. Also grooming the dog's coat is another important point in showing.

HOW TO REGISTER YOUR DOG

Whether you intend to show or not, it is always advisable to register your dog at the Kennel Club. The more so if you intend to breed from him or her. If it is intended to exhibit the dog then, of course, it becomes compulsory to register; otherwise you cannot make your entries. The cost of registration is small, the fee being 2/6 per dog. Forms of application with full particulars, will be sent free if you apply to :-

Holland Buckley, Esq., Secretary, Kennel Club,
84, Piccadilly, London W.1.

All registrations are published monthly in the official organ, *The Kennel Gazette.*

DOG PAPERS

There are two specialist dog papers, dealing entirely with dogs, these being *Our Dogs* and *The Dog World.* They carry announcements concerning all the dog shows, and a postcard to any Secretary of any selected Club or Society will bring schedules, entry forms, and Kennel Club registration forms by return post.

SALE

Puppies, Stud Dogs, Brood Bitches, supplied to suit all requirements, whether it be for Show, Sport, Guard or Companion, I will supply you. Animals exported to all part of the world.

JACK BARNARD

BRONZE MODEL OF A FIGHTING DOG IN THE MID
19TH CENTURY

INTRODUCTION

"Red Gentleman of Staffordshire" reprinted from "Neither Man nor Dog" by Gerald Kersh, Esq., by kind permission of the publishers, William Heinemann, Ltd. Below I wish to give my readers a view of the true courage, faith, stamina, guts and tenacity of a true Staffordshire, this little story goes to prove the faith put into mankind by our Canine Pals, yet this love and courage is abused by some types of individuals for filthy *lucre*. However this type of sport, I am delighted to say is dead or very fast dying, but the above only goes to prove the yeoman stock our present Dogs are bred from, therefore as previously mentioned, to see a true Staffordshire crawling on his belly in the ring is really nauseating to a lover of this grand old breed, especially a person who has known the breed for many years.

RED GENTLEMAN OF
STAFFORDSHIRE
Could I be less than a dog?
by Gerald Kersh

I saw Gavin Eld a twelve weeks after he got back. He used to have the kind of head a five-year old child could portray in ten seconds - a jug-handled lopsided oval enclosing a couple of arches over a pair of dots, representing eyes and brows; an O for a nose and an almost straight line intended to be a mouth. But in the eleven months of his absence something had been at work on his chalky sketch of a face: in one or two great strokes it had been marked with a power, a calm and a certain dignity. It takes anguish to do that. Pain strengthens the face as weight lifting strengthens the body ... provided you do not compel yourself to carry more than you were made to bear.

Yes, some masterhand had shaded him, giving him weight and depth. And something else had tried to deface him. His forehead and left cheek were scribbled over with scars. Eld still grinned his rabbit tooth grin, but in a lopsided way, and behind eyes, which had been expressionless as grey glass marbles that used to cork lemonade bottles when the world was young, there was a strange shadow, Suffering had thinned him. His skin looked burnt, and hung loose : he walked with a sort of wolfish lope.

Mine was the only face he knew when he came into camp. He had little enough to say ... that he had been captured at Louvaine but got away. For forty weeks Gavin Eld had been on the fun in dangerous territory, eating and sleeping like an hunted beast in gulps and snatches under hedges and in shadowy doorways. About Eld's headlong assault against a thousand miles of fantastic distance, there was something crazy and wonderful : it had the madness and the grandeur of the charge of Bohemund's God-intoxicated men at Antioch. Hopelessly lost, quite alone on the gloomy plains of France, he had walked home. He was convinced that the war was lost. He wanted to get back to die. France and Belgium had slid into the depths like shale off a cliff. Eld found himself stumbling in the débris of a great grey ruin. He knew that he had travelled eastwards, so he walked westwards.

I asked him : "What did you eat?"

He said : "What I could get."

"Where did you sleep?"

"Where I lay down."

They gave him a Military Medal. He drew twenty-five pounds of back pay. One week, or fifteen pounds later, I saw him in a cocktail bar in Woking. He was sitting on a red leather stool sipping mild ale. Next to him sat a sulphur-headed woman in slacks holding a lead attached to a bull terrier. Eld was staring at this dog with gloomy eyes. When he saw me he said, in an audible whisper, jerking a careless thumb : "Great fat cowardly bitch."

The woman said : "I beg your pardon?"

Eld said : "I mean the dog, lady, not thee. She'll weigh forty-eight pounds, give or take a pound?"

"I don't know, I'm sure."

Eld said : "I lay five pounds she's fast."

"Fast?"

"Ay ... fast to come, fast to go. If she was mine I'd put her in a sack wi' a stone, and chuck her in t' Cut."

"Oh, you would, would you?"

"Lady," said Eld, "I know dogs. It was me as owned Skylarks. That's foreign for Tearer."

"*Scylax*," I said.

"Ay, Tearer by name, Tearer by nature. Bitch's choice, and the greatest dog ever pupped."

"Greyhound?" asked the sulphur-headed blonde.

"No lady, a put dog."

"A pit dog? I've heard of pit ponies - "

"Lady," said Gavin Eld, "a Staffordshire bull terrier, lady a fighting dog, lady, a killer. The greatest battler that ever breathed, a red dog, a real Staffordshire bull, a pit dog, a proper gentleman of Staffordshire. "

"I'm afraid I don't quite understand."

"A fighting dog, lady, a thirty-pound fighter. He could kill anything God stood on four legs, or know the reason why. He saved me twice."

I believe that Gavin Eld must have drunk a lot of mild ale. He was never a talker. But he talked now. We edged away from the bar and sat at a table. I remember that the woman in slacks came with us, followed by her great, square chested bull terrier. Eld felt it's neck and sneered. "Skylarks would have taken her guts out in seven minutes," he said. "That was a dog. That was a dog of the old fighting breed. You or I, Gerald, couldn't wish to have a better father and mother. And he saved me twice.

Then he told us. I shall not try to reproduce his strange, ugly nasal-throaty accent. Once in a while he dropped into slang. The blonde stared at him fascinated. I did too. He began to talk about fighting dogs; and as he talked I swear to you that there crept into my nostrils a strange, acrid smell of dogs and beer and tobacco smoke and the small hours ... I seemed to see a public house parlour in the Midlands ... Men were waiting : leather faced men with clamped mouths, eleven or twelve of them; and about six dogs ... little dogs, with a certain viperish triangularity of head, a doggedness of jaw, a peculiar width between the eyes. I tell you that I saw it and I smelt it.

Perhaps you associate the dog fight with ancient history. But dogs still fight. The ancient breed of the fighting dog is still maintained; the descendants of the crop-eared bear-baiters are still bred - terrible dogs, good for nothing but mortal combat, but shockingly good for that. They mate them, still, in the North of England and the Midlands : Staffordshire Terriers that would rather fight than eat. I had often wondered what Gavin Eld had done for his living. In that absurd cocktail bar as he sat with the sulphur blonde on his left and me on his right, he seemed to peel himself off. He stripped off his present life like a plaster.

He talked.

Skylarks was a great dog. His father was great, and his mother was a great bitch. You don't know the Staffordshire bull. He is a wonderful dog. It's an instinct of women, and other she animals, to protect the weakest of a litter. (Haven't you seen how a woman will stand by a humpy backed child?). But a Staffordshire bitch will choose, always, the finest fighting dog of the litter. You called him *Scylax*. I meant to

23

call him that, but I never had your education. I called him Skylarks. He was a great dog - ginger as a chorus girl, cobby, balanced like scales and - so to speak - almost hanging in mid air. He was a great fighter, and he saved me twice.

I dare say you know that I get my living, when I get my living, out of dogs. I keep 'em and I breed 'em. I breed only fighters and killers. I have had one dog that got me £350 a year for two years. He was killed. He was a Staffordshire bull and it was a Staffordshire bull that killed him : his throat was torn out after a fight that lasted one hour and forty-eight minutes.

I had Skylark's mother for a long time. Skylark was out of her by Ripper. They were red and he was red - a very red dog indeed, ginger as they come. You know, I dare say, how you train one of them bulls ... you wear heavy boots and kick them, toe up. No need to go into details. I will tell you all you want to know : only two things are needed to train a Staffordshire bull - heavy nailed boots and a steel bar. They don't feel nothing else.

I trained Skylark's for fighting. When he was a mere puppy I chucked him in a fighting mongrel, and watched Skylarks kill him and take out his liver and eat it. Soon I lived on that dog. I can't tell you what he looked like : I can only tell you some points. Give or take a pound, he weighted thirty pounds and was red. He had a head like a coal scuttle, a little tiny tail and a stocky body. As it so happened, he was born with cropped ears. I have not known this to happen before. His ears needed no crop. Everything that you can imagine in the way of fight, all that you ever thought of in the way of guts and courage was in that dog. At three months he would have fought a lion.

I trained him; I trained him as I never trained a dog in my life before or since. Ah! Nothing in the world, lady, nothing in the world, Gerald, can come up to a good Staffordshire bull - a good pit dog of breed. There's blood there! Give me blood! Against all the world, give me breed and blood; because if you produce a little naked rat that's got blood and breed, he'll fight, although his soul is bigger than his body.

24

But Skylarks. This was a dog. For over a year and a half I lived on him, and I'll swear to you by the soul of my father and mother that I loved him like a brother. You may not believe it, but in those eighteen months he won thirty fights. Not a dog that stood against him lived to brag about it, except one - a lemon coloured dog - whose master threw in the towel. Tearer by name, tearer by nature. He would run in, stop in, hold, kill, come out wagging his little tail and sleep. I used to take him to the pit in a pram with my kid. That dog that would have fought like a leopard - ay, by God, and killed him or died - he would lie down next to the kid, holding his little hand between his teeth and never dreaming of hurting him. That is your fighting dog, your Staffordshire bull. A swine with anything on four legs, but a lamb with a child.

Well ... I ran into some trouble and, worse than ever in my life, I wanted some money. Now Skylarks was a great dog, and everybody in the world knew him as such. I would have backed Skylarks with everything I ever possessed against any beast that ever had a leg in every corner of itself. But I couldn't get a match; and there was a certain party called Joe Blue that wanted to buy Skylarks off me for twenty pounds. I dare say you know one can get to like a dog. I wouldn't sell. And then the brokers came in and I went to Joe Blue and said I'd sell; but he wouldn't buy. He offered me ten; and I spat on it.

He said : "Look. I'll tell you what. How much have you got?"
"A fiver," I said.
He said, lady ... Gerald, he said : "Will you match him against two Alsatians?"
I said : "Yes."

And so I took Skylarks along to meet Blue's Alsatians. You know that Alsatian. He runs in and slashes. Blue had a dog and a bitch. Skylarks killed the dog in a minute and a half, and the bitch had slashed him to ribbons and they were locked jaw to jaw. Skylarks had the sense of a man. You know, when two dogs are fighting, how you take them apart - the dog that has the hold, you push him forward and then pull him back. Skylarks manoeuvred himself loose like a Christian and got a hold on a pinch of skin in the Alsatian's throat, and shifted, and got a proper grip, and killed her. By God, my God, that dear little dog ... he was a warrior

25

and he was a gentleman and God send us all a heart like the heart there was in that dog! It was all over in five and three quarter minutes, and Skylarks was standing by me, and I was dabbing peroxide of hydrogen on his cuts. Because he was cut, that lovely dog - he was cut up like macaroni. I collected my stakes. Then Blue said :

> "Do you want to make yourself, or lose yourself some month?"
> "What way?" I said.
> Blue said : "He holds."
> I said : "In life or death."

Then Blue said something horrible. He said :"He was holding with his jaw nearly broke. Do you think he'd hold with a leg cut off?"

I said : How do you mean?"
He said : I'll lay you thirty pounds to ten he'd drop his hold of an iron bar if I took off a paw with an axe.

I thought. I was disgusted, because as I said, I had a liking for that dog. But then again, the brokers were in, the lass was sick and a kid was coming. I said to Skylarks : "Skylarks, brother, brother dog, brother Skylarks, I like you and I don't want to do it to you ... but Skylarks, I've got to do it. Skylarks" I said, "I'd sooner cut off my own paw. But nobody will lay a bet on that because I'm a man, and you're a dog. But Skylarks, forgive me, I got to do it because t' old lass wants t'brass and there's a kid coming. So make ready and lay hold."

He understood. They held up a bar and he laid hold like I told him. And then Blue took off his fore-paw with an axe, and that dog, that red dog, that lovely gentleman, he still kept hold; and I collected my money, and I cried like a child.

I fought him again on three legs, and another red dog, a fine red dog, killed him. And on another bet - although it broke my heart to see him there - we opened him, and let God by my judge, three minutes after he was dead ... in-out, in-out in-out, his heart was still beating.

My lovely Skylarks, my beautiful little Staffordshire gentleman! I wish he had been my father or my son. A man has a duty but I loved him; I tell you that I loved him better than the old lass and better than the kid that came. I'd change anything. I'd give anything for him back.

And when I broke away and I was lying there, dying ... dying of hunger, hunger and cold and misery out in those plains, lying in a ditch ...

... Do you know what it's like to dream of hunger? When your belly is eating itself up because there is nothing left for it to eat? You dream of waves, of a sort of fog in waves like a misty day; only it moves like a sea and carries you with it ... and when you wake up you're sick, and cold, and you want to give up. I'm telling you something. I would have given up a dozen times in them months, lady. Yes Gerald, I would have given up time and time again ... only I kept thinking about Skylarks. That lovely red Staffordshire gentleman. And I ask you - could I be less than a dog? He was better than most things : but he was a dog, only a dog. And I'm a man. Could I be less? So I broke through in the end .

Gavin Eld made rings on the table with his glass. He was speaking in an undertone now, like a man alone and talking to himself. Had the beer overtaken him?

He muttered :

"That fight na more, my red beauty; thalt ne'er fly in agen at t'enemy's throat with tha grad heart of iron banging lak a drum a glow in tha black een lak calls. I'll not feel tha bull's neck in my hands, nay, never agen, never. Eh, tha wicked swine, nobbut death'd separate t'enemy and thee, and tha shamed me back to life. Ay, tha didst, tha knows tha didst ... and but for remembering thee I'd a' gone back lak a coward. Thoroughbred to t' bone as thart, could I let thee think tha master was nobbut a cur?"

Then he rose, not very steadily. "He was only a dog," he said. "But I'm only a man."

27

Much water has passed under the bridges since the birth of "The Staffordshire Bull Terrier Club" which was recognised by the Kennel Club in 1935, and the first entries in the register were published in the May issue of the Kennel Gazette, the following being a copy of the entry, by kind permission of Kennel Club.

(1) "Black Sultan" Dog. Mr. A. Wade, S. Jack, D. Gyp. Breeder Mr. L. Robinson. Whelped September 22-33.

(2) "Brindle Duchess" Bitch, Mr. A. Smith, S. The Nut. D. Ladysmith, Breeder Owner. Whelped 31-8-33.

(3) "Camocles" Dog, Mr. H. J. Lloyd, Pedigree unknown. Breeder Mr. W. Smith. Whelped 31-6-31.

(4) "Rum Major of Rum" Dog, Mr. T. D. King, S. Dan. D. Floss. Breeder Mr. A. Jeavons. Whelped 10-8-34.

(5) "Buller of Torfield" Dog, Mrs. R. Raine Barker, S. Buster D. Bother. Breeder T. Walls, Esq. Whelped 22-9-34.

(6) "Woodgate Sanco" Dog. Mrs. M. Smith, Jnr. S. Pilot. D. Lady. Breeder Mr. S. D. Poole. Whelped 1-9-34.

This making a grand total of six and yet to see the total Registrations for 1949 which was approximately 3,000, makes one really think that the old adage to be very true, namely "That Saints were made from small beginnings, so History repeat itself". The foundation was laid, and strength mounts upon strength and time marches on with vast improvements a register for the Staffordshire Bull Terrier was opened as a result of a decision of the committee of the Kennel Club on May 17th, 1938, and prior to that time Staffordshire Bull Terriers had been registered under the any other Breed or Variety Register.

The first Staffordshires to obtain the proud honour of "Champion" was Mr. Joe Mallens "Gentleman Jim" and Mr. Joe Dennis "Lady Eve". Both becoming full Champions the same day at the same show, namely Bath Championship Show, 4th May, 1939. In passing I must mention the name of my friend and colleague Joe Dunn, in my opinion this gentleman has done as much as any man alive today to give the Stafford its true and correct place in Dogdom the love where it rightly belongs. I say without any hesitation that he is also recognised as one of

28

"CHESTONION NIBS PAL"

the authorities and his services in this respect are widely sought. At the first Club Show held by the Staffordshire Bull Terrier Club at the Conservative Club, Cradley Heath, on 17th August, 1935, our old dog "Jim-the-Dandy" was awarded Best Dog in Show, being Judged by that well known authority of the Breed H.N. Beilby, Esq. Also another honour held by our Kennels, is that we were the first to export a Staffordshire as a pure breed since recognition by Kennel Club, this being the Crufts Winning Bitch "Shell-of-Gold", who was exported to New York, U.S.A. Since this happened the "Chestonions" have gone to very many corners of the world.

Although Dog fighting is abolished in this country same is very prevalent in America and below I give you my readers a little write up of only a few months ago.

"A few lines about Mr. Leunnes "Big Jack of Gardis", Miss U.S.A. Well let us see what Mr. Leunnes has to say about his Dog "Big Jack" his famous Pit Bull Terrier, Mr. Leunnes is one of the best known fanciers of the Pit Bull Terrier in America and has owned bred and fought very many good dogs, he being in the game purely for sport and pleasure and only goes in for Breeding and owning the very gamest of the game. Following is a description of "Big Jack" Leunnes Jack was a fifty five lbs Dog and was classed as the Champion of North America at his weight, Jack was a combination of the Gas House Dog and Burkes imported Rafferty Dog, he imported him W. J. Farren of St. John, N.B. Canada, he was a terrible punisher, in fact, old time dog men, claim he was without a doubt the greatest fighting Dog of this age. He killed Farren's Tim in forty seven minutes, killed Powers Bob in forty nine minutes, licked Poole's Dog "Decatur" Alabama in sixteen minutes, stopped "Rowdy" of New Orleans, who had been expressly brought from Brooklyn N.Y. to defeat him in eighteen minutes, stopped Faulkner's "Duke" Tallahatchie in twenty seven minutes, and was open against all comers for any amount for four years, without a taker.

Mrs. Leunnes won nineteen straight money fights without a defeat.

30

A lot of people call it cruel, but gloat and smile when Atomic bombs wipe out the whole population of an entire city, this being the explanation of Dog fighting in U.S.A.

I do without a doubt like to see a Stafford with the essential spirit and characteristic of the breed. But I am afraid, and I will go so far as to say the majority of our present day issue, are lacking this spirit. Guts having been forgotten and a thing of the past, what looks more daft than a silly Stafford' especially to one who knows a Stafford. However here's hoping we may keep the flag flying and breed, uphold and maintain the vital essentials to our good old breed. I am not advocating a raving maniac, but I do maintain and uphold that to see a Stafford in the ring, crawling on its belly, utterly terrified, is enough to make a true sportsmen utterly disgusted, so I do appeal to all owners and breeders to try and maintain that true essential in the Stafford, namely spirit. Since our standard was drawn up in 1935 some has been revised whether to the good or detriment of the breed I refuse to say, but I will say here and now that a 16 inch dog weighing 36-40 lbs to my mind is silly, the Terrier characteristic being displaced by a Bull Dog type of animal, such is the modern requirements, however the least said on this subject the better.

In my booklet I am trying to give the novice both by photographs and literature the true outline of what a really good Staffordshire is like and should any of you dear readers ever be in doubt, never fail to write me and if at all possible to give you advice, assistance or guidance over any matter, I shall be only too pleased to assist in whatever you would like to know, so never be afraid of getting in touch with me, I do maintain and uphold that I have been seriously associated in dogs during the past 30 years and not 30 months, and I may add that I have been associated with dogs from the cradle, but up to the age of 18/20, I never took things too serious owing to study, etc., from this age onwards, I may add, Dogs apart from my business have been a part of my life and always will be I suppose. I would like to say the two main Clubs in the Country today are the Parent Club, namely, "The Staffordshire Bull Terrier Club" and "The Southern Counties Staffordshire Bull Terrier Club", these I feel sure being the two leading light, although several more are in existence and also as far afield as Scotland and Ireland. I now feel confident, that any one after perusing these columns and also having a sight of some of the finest arrivals in the

31

country, will, in his or her own mind know the value of a true Staffordshire. Believe me readers when I say, if need by, your Staffordshire would gladly go to his death with a smile for you, so great is his love for master or mistress and all he asks is your kindness in return, the dog always has and always will find a sure and certain place and in return all he asks for is, "in health" proper food, "in sickness" proper attention, always proper accommodation and above all proper environment, this my dear reader is not a big request and in return there is his warm whole hearted love that is given blindly, asking no reward, seeing no faults unfaltering always, the dog looks to man for his ALL, he is never his own Master, his own Chef, his own Doctor or his own Architect, he is to be always fed, tended and housed by man and to prosper or to suffer according to the knowledge of his master. Therefore I strongly appeal to any who may read these words to study and help in the life of perhaps his or her most faithful and truest friend in LIFE, and thus accompanied, the person will perhaps appreciate their dog the more, but not nearly so much as the dog will in return appreciate his master.

"THE GREAT BOMBER"
The property of Joe Mallen, Esq.

CHAMPION GENTLEMAN JIM"
The property of Joe Mallen, Esq.

JOE MALLEN, ESQ.

It is with great pleasure that I pen these few lines about my old pal and colleague Joe Mallen. I know he will forgive me, but I say here and now without any hesitation whatsoever that I yet have to see the man who can condition a Stafford better than Joe. Whenever I have judged, it has always been a pleasure to me to go over his dogs, their condition always reminded me of a fighting fit boxer ready to enter the ring. In my humble opinion, the finest dog he ever owned was "The Great Bomber" a really beautiful animal of superb quality and had the late war not of intervened with showing, this dog could have been a champion over and over again and gone from success to success. The outstanding champion from these kennels was that great stalwart of the breed the late "Champion Gentleman Jim", this dog I may add has played a great part in Staffordshire Bull Terrier history and the majority of pedigrees one peruses, you will more or less find champion "Gentleman Jim". This animal I may add was the first dog in the breed to gain the coveted title of Champion and his third and final certificate to give him this honour was obtained at the Bath Show on 4th May 1939.

Should space allow I could no doubt write a full book on this sportsman and his dogs, and I go so far as to say that here we have a man who has been cradled with a Stafford and nor a couple of years experience as a Judge of the breed, his services are widely sought and I conclude with saying that he will go out of his way to assist the novice.

"CHAMPION WIDNEYLAND KIM"
The property of Gerald A. Dudley, Esq.

"CHAMPION WYCHBURY KIMBO"
The property of Gerald A. Dudley, Esq.

37

"CHAMPION WYCHBURY PIED WONDER"
The property of Gerald A. Dudley, Esq.

38

GERALD A. DUDLEY, ESQ.

It gives me great pleasure to state that I have known Gerald A. Dudley, Esq., for some 20 years and I say without hesitation that this gentleman is the King Pin of exhibitors at the present time, he is honour bound to feel extremely proud owning no fewer than seven full champions, a world record for any one owner in Staffordshire Bull Terriers, Mr. Dudley I may add has been very interested in Staffords, I should say about 25 years, this being a Criterion to his knowledge and also giving him full knowledge of what his aims and ambitions are, at the formation of the Staffordshire Bull Terrier Club, when I was honoured with the first presidency, our friend Gerald exhibited at the first and second show with degrees of success. He has taken great interest in all Midland and other Clubs where Staffords have been shown and possibly as very many of the older generation of Staffordshire exhibitors know was a founder member of the Midland Counties Bull Breeds, being elected its President during the last three years, and also has held the Presidency of the Staffordsrhire Bull Terrier Club. Some of his stock at the present moment include, Champion "Widneyland Kim", Champion "Wychbury Kimbo", Champion "Jims Double of Wychbury" Champion "Brindle Crescendo of Wychbury". In dogs and in bitches, Champion "Wychbury Red Cap", Champion "Wychbury Oak Beauty", Champion Pied Wonder". When viewing these Kennels for my write up I was greatly impressed with every animal I saw, as each and all had the vital essential to a Stafford, to be vulgar, guts, stock which are not game have a short stay at these kennels as our friend likes to uphold and maintain a reputation of the true Staffordshire tradition and character.

Items gained in the Show Ring which stand as records are namely :-

(a)   Champion "Wychbury Red Cap" was the very first Staffordshire puppy to gain a Challenge Certificate, this honour being gained at the age of 9 1/2 months, her second Certificate being gained on her 1st birthday and a full Champion at 13 1/2 months of age, the youngest Staffordshire Champion ever.

(b)   On two occasions he has won both dog and bitch Certificates at the same Championship Show, I awarded him this honour, when I judged the "Southern Counties" Championship Show in London giving "Oak Beauty" her third and final certificate, and in dogs to "Jims Double of Wychbury".

(c)   On seven occasions have won a Challenge Certificate and Reserve Challenge Certificate at the same show.

(d)   Both Dog and Bitch Champion Brindles.
Both Dog and Bitch Champion Reds.
Both Dog and Bitch Champion Pieds.

These are records that have made history and I say with the fullest of sincerity will be very hard to emulate by any one Breeder of the Champion dogs housed in these kennels. I have heard very many heated arguments and I am inclined to believe the owner that the king pin of the bunch is that dark Brindle "Champion Widneyland Kim". Many upholding he being the finest champion son of the greatest pillar of the breed. The late Champion "Gentleman Jim" "Kim" I may add is the sire of Champion "Wychbury Kimbo" and Champion "Wychbury Pied Wonder" also challenge Certificate winners "Tessas Pride" "Shanghi Lil" "Garland of Pyecode" many Reserve C.C. Winners and best in show winners.

Of Champion Wychbury Kimbo I must add that this very worthy son of "Kim" has the distinguished honour of never having known defeat in his career, having gained 33 Red cards and his Three Challenge Certificates off the mark and really marvellous performance and one I would say very hard to emulate of Champion "Wychbury Pied Wonder" a really smashing daughter of "Kim" I would say a marvellous bitch. She qualified for her full title at five outings, she as a beautiful pear shaped head, wonderful spring of rib and is in my opinion one of the finest bitches on show today, of this gentleman and his dogs I could confine my booklet, but space will now allow for such, but I will conclude by saying that my friend will go out of his way to help and assist professional or novice, any club or society, even at his own personal expense, so what more can a person do for the Breed or individual.

40

"CHAMPION "FEARLESS-RED-OF-BANDITS"
The property of John F. Gordon, Esq.

"CHAMPION LUCKY STAR OF BANDITS"
The property of Mrs. M. Gordon and Mr. E. R. Davies.

41

"CHAMPION BRIGANDS RED ROGERSON"
The property of John F. Gordon, Esq.

JOHN F. GORDON ESQ.

Of the younger generation, I say without any hesitation whatsoever that Mr. John F. Gordon, of the "Bandits" Kennels is one of the leading lights in the Staffordshire Fancy, and I would say the most prominent in the south, as these Kennels have the honour of housing no fewer than three champions, no mean objective, namely Champion "Fearless Red of Bandits" Champion "Brigands Red Rogerson" Champion "Lucky Star of Bandits". In passing, I may add that I had the pleasure of awarding this gentleman his first Challenge Certificate to that renowned sire "Fearless Red" and needless to say the other two Certificates quickly followed giving him the proud title of Champion, next to gain this full title was that outstanding little animal Champion "Brigands Red Rogerson" no doubt the outstanding light weight dog in the breed today.

Next to follow in line was "Lucky Star of Bandits" a beautiful pied bitch, I had the pleasure of awarding this bitch her second Certificate, this bitch also has the honour of having been best exhibit in show All Breeds at Hertfordshire C.S. Open Show, under that well known authority Austin Hollingworth, Esq. The Kennels of Mr. Gordon are expertly conducted as a recreation and pleasure by himself and his very able assistant Mrs. Marjorie Gordon, herself a Specialist Judge and a very keen horse woman.

Every animal at these kennels is expertly conditioned, with health, soundness and true type joining hand in hand with correct Staffordshire temperament, for this is a breed in which nervousness is Anathema. Mr. Gordon is too well known as a Championship Judge for me to pass any comments and is also the *Dog World* Breed Correspondent. During the past year, stock from these Kennels have been exported to about fifteen different parts of the world. In conclusion I may add that Mr. and Mrs. Gordon will always be very pleased to welcome any visitors to their Kennels and needless to say their expert advice and guidance is always to be given, especially to the novice just on the threshold of starting to commence a Kennel.

"WIDNEYLAND LITTLE GENT OF PYNEDALE"
The property of Arthur Payton Smith, Esq.

"CHAMPION BRIGANDS BO'SUN"
The property of Arthur Payton Smith, Esq.

ARTHUR PAYTON SMITH, ESQ.

Arthur Payton Smith, Esq., is too well known in Staffordshire Bull Terriers to make any comment, one of the leading exhibitors today and success has followed success to give this gentleman and his kennels the reputation they have, today. One of the leading lights in this kennel, is that pillar of the breed Champion "Brigands Bosun" prior to advent of championship Shows, owing to the misfortune of war, he was many times best in show, all breeds apart from Staffordshires, when over five years old he won his first Challenge Certificate at Leicester in 1948, and I had the pleasure of awarding him his third and final one at the Cardiff Championship Show in May 1949, thus giving him the proud title of champion.

Some of his stock include "Wychbury Red Cap", 3 C.Cs. "Thornhill Pride" 3 C.Cs., 1 Res. C.C., "Widneyland Ritver Ringleader " 4 C.Cs., 2 Res. C.Cs., "Widneyland Brutus" 2 C.Cs., the late "Brindle Daisy" 2 C.Cs., 4 Res. C.Cs. Other winners by this grand animal are far too numerous to mention, he is still in great demand for stud, as the former information only goes to prove that like begets like.

An outstanding young dog in these kennels is "Widneyland Little Gent of Pynedale" a really beautiful son of that grand specimen of the breed Champion "Wychbury Kimbo". Little Gent I may add came Reserve C.C. at thirteen months old and also has the honour of being the first Stafford to win a stakes class at a Championship Show, this honour being attained at the Kensington Championship Show 1949, also having won the Kennel Club junior warrant, I have no hesitation in saying that this grand young dog is due for top honours, and I feel confident that he can and will emulate some of the famous Dogs houses in these kennels.

Payton Smith has been in Staffordshire for quite a number of years and his only aim in life is to breed and exhibit only the very best possible. This reputation he upholds and maintains and anyone interested in viewing his stock are always given a real Staffordshire welcome. In conclusion I may add that Mr. Smith is the proud possessor of that noted Boxer Champion "Lustig of Gerdas Hosftee". Mr. Smith is recognised as one of our leading Championship Show Judges both in Staffordshire Bull Terriers and Boxers.

"BIRCHES BARROW BOY"
The property of Alf. Lewis, Esq.

ALF. LEWIS, ESQ.

Mr. Alf Lewis, a newcomer to the ranks of Staffordshire Bull Terriers has the correct idea and outlook of the breed and is the proud possessor of that grand young Red Dog "Birches' Barrow Boy". This animal has only been exhibited at Two Championship Shows, namely Olympia, under that world wide Staffordshire Bull Terrier authority, Joe Dunn, Esq., who awarded him Four Firsts. Following this success his next venture was Crufts, where he never ought to have been exhibited, as he had only just recovered from an illness, and was not in condition. Yet even under these poor conditions, he obtained One Second and Reserve in the Open Dog Class. This was no mean attainment for a dog not properly conditioned. These awards were obtained under that world wide authority, Leo Wilson, Esq.

Mr. Lewis's idea is very sound, as he knows what he wants and I may endorse the remarks by saying "that he is on the correct track, type, soundness and symmetry being his ambition, combined with that true 'Staffordshire Spirit' absolutely necessary in this Breed of Dog. I venture to go so far as to say this dog is bound to make a name for himself, as he is in the hands of a person who neither considers time or distance as long as he gets a fair crack of the whip, taking on all comers under any judge of repute.